Let's Go Dancing in the Light

A Collection of Poetry and Prose for Soul and Spirit

Gloria D. Gonsalves

authorHOUSE®

AuthorHouse™ UK
1663 Liberty Drive
Bloomington, IN 47403 USA
www.authorhouse.co.uk
Phone: 0800.197.4150

Published by AuthorHouse   05/17/2017

ISBN: 978-1-5246-8115-9 (sc)
ISBN: 978-1-5246-8125-8 (e)

Contents

A Prologue: On Religion And My Writing

There have been occasions where some of my readers confronted me regarding my religious denomination. My response has been and continues to be, "Did you see a religious criterion to read any of my writing?"

Religion should not be about converting or judging others. I would like to think that as humans we need to give each other the freedom to grow spiritually from any religious faith. Each one of us connects with a higher power in a way that makes sense to us, whether through Jesus, Muhammad, Yogananda, Buddha, archangels, etc. Therefore, my faith, your faith and their faith should not hinder us from treating each other with respect and love.

My messages are focused in inspiring readers regardless of their religious background. Sometimes I may lean more towards my Christian faith. This should not be translated that I want you to become one. It only means that I can express myself better that way. Also, I grew up in Tanzania, where all religious faiths are embraced with respect. The country's public holidays include Christian and Muslim celebrations. As such, I do not hesitate to acknowledge lessons from other religious groups to help me grow spiritually.

As a reader, I thank you for understanding and respecting one another regardless of our religious background.

In Search Of Liberty

Angry was not an option
so I became docile and timid.

Fanning and watching
from a secluded distance.

Scrolling through papers
which dismiss my kind.

Meeting and speaking
in the tones of pretence.

Nodding and agreeing
to the ideas made for me.

Slicing and rolling food
in praise of others' etiquette.

Inventing and supporting
reasons for injustice.

Existing in silent inertia
to not rock the boat.

Writing was an option
so I became a truthteller.

Write Your Defense

Be assured, child of silenced voice,
imprudent words thrown at you as trash
serve as treasure of your glorious living.

Collect them with humility of a star
about to sign a celebrated publication
of alphabets that made you an outcast.

Don't succumb to revenge lowliness
or destructive melancholy of despair,
but jottings of ascending notable being.

With each spit of careless harshness
shield your pride with pen and paper
to emerge resilient in chapters of life.

Be a stalwart of good from bad torments
command your ink to own sacred virtues
until divine text extinguishes their malice.

Write, erase and re-write your burden
until it is words of fearless and spirited
refining ridicule to bodacious meaning.

Ten Questions

Who invented idea of religions? And why
can't we all pray to the same God? Is it bad
to share same worshipping house?
Why do humans get caught up in their own
faith? A sip of wine? Will I really be damned
to hell for drinking? If so, where did grapes come
from? Sex perhaps? Is it a sin to have a
wet dream? Can I glorify God through any of these?

I watched them
hypnotised with prayers
promising obedience
and a life without fault.

They scorned
at one who prayed not.
But the faithless
is life full of giving.

They keep praying
and promising
and scorning.

The sinner
is living
and giving
a hope
which life
takes gratefully.

The God we pray to
can't be this agathokakological.

Tell me which God
amputates children as victory,
kills to amplify the holy word.

This same God
creates children in his image,
commands 'you shall not murder'.

Our Pact

In the name of our ancestors,
ourselves and future generations
I will meet you half way.
Your aggression will be erased
from my heart and mind
to free our souls and spirits.
Take, this day, my hand
and promise to absolve
what my forefathers and I did
to you and your kin.
Surrender not
into brutal deliberations
for the sake of our peoples' peace.
Intend forgiveness today
as I seek it with introspection.
Accept this as our pact
and the beginning of our healing.

If We Were All Heretics

There wouldn't be Gods and Goddesses
or books lowering the holiness of human.
There wouldn't be flocks adoring the deities
or verses proclaiming humans as sinners.
There wouldn't be righteous and wicked
or commands casting off dissimilar ideology.
There wouldn't be rules on how to pray
or guidelines to seek the divine in ourselves.
There wouldn't be if we were all heretics.

The Futuristic Prayer

In the name of you, and you, and you, I came.
Give yourself a break from any holy book; and
start looking at others as you want to be looked at.
Forget the temptation to revisit the taught morals
and seek to free yourself from judgement of idols.
For your kingdom is that what you carry within
ennobled by your presence as you, and you, and you.
Now and then.

In the world of light and dark
kingdoms of noble pen scribble
a struggle to crown the faith book.

Some ink drown in peasant blood
whose words exhale cursed fire
of incest between verse and prose.

Marked with gloom hatched as ice
blown by bitter winds of sad days
theirs is art of a banned scripture.

The truth chronicled in hiding
doomed to remain a book of words
unpublished in the war of faith.

You read, "Spirituality is for those who have been to hell and are seeking heaven". The sentence attracted you. There must be something else other than religion that will nurture a relationship with your divine self. This something will help guide your spirit without seeming like a crowd control in a choreographed Sunday mass.

It was a hot July day when you were introduced to the oldest church in the Amsterdam's main red-light district. It was in this church that you recalled the fearful voices of others throughout your life. "You cannot study art. You cannot discuss sex matters. You cannot touch yourself. You cannot remain single. You cannot marry a man of another tribe or religion. You cannot be married and have no children. You cannot count on an adopted child as your own. You cannot trust a man. You cannot divorce. You cannot question the cultural practices. You cannot be a believer and not attend a mass. You cannot have two faiths. You cannot wear trousers to work or church. You cannot speak against homophobia. You cannot…" The list of cannots made your head buzz with doubts about yourself. You craved to have a list of own dos which nourished your spirit.

What if you went ahead and have inappropriate thoughts about the greatest Michael? And through him commit your first sacred sex. Perhaps all these fears and worries would be gone. His sword of light would unbind you from all anxieties and reveal the glorious female you are supposed to be. The Angelus gong reminded that you were in God's house. You stopped thinking about your forbidden encounter with strong Michael. Days later, this forbidden thought gave you courage. You began having a relationship not only with Michael but other celestial beings. You studied them and knew by heart whom to call for what situation. Even when at intimacy, you knew if you called the one responsible for joy, you would have the best time of your divine body.

Today you keep both your given religious faith and discovered spirituality. Faith connects you with the rest of humanity while spirituality connects you with yourself. But you know it is not enough. You want to also understand what other religious faiths than yours have. You keep hoping that someday doors to all holy houses will be open for everyone to enter. That welcoming gesture will end the lunacy of justifying holiness based on comparisons and condemnations. All the imposed fears and judgements on others and ourselves will stop. And then a memory of light will be triggered. We all are different spiritual with the same source of divine light. May these words be.

There's no year.
There's no finish line.
There's no alternative.
There's no utopia.
There's no internet.
There's no cat.
There's no doctor.
There's no debt crisis.
There's no religion.
There's no enemy.
There's no now.
There's no tomorrow.
There's no future.
There's no word.
There's no such thing.

Would we want a calendar?
Would we stop bustling?
Would we start talking?
Would we reclaim patience?
Would we love our bodies?
Would we have no allergies?
Would we end social categories?
Would we share freely?
Would we cheer for each other?
Would we accept our differences?
Would we be tolerant?
Would we end wars?
Would we feel free?
Would we hate nothing?
Would we love everything?

The perfume of orange blossoms invited you to sit down in the middle of a strange farm. You sighted a mud hut outlined by the evening light to a golden sight which you had only seen in paintings. You picked an orange and smelled it. Then you scratched its peel with your manicured finger and smelled it again. You kept scratching and smelling that fruit as if it were a scent operating your breathing. Then you began marvelling and questioning, as you always do.

Why was it considered lowly, being a manual labourer? Why creating has gotten so much attention compared to inventing? Why TV shows don't portray farming in an elegant form as it did with creative arts? Why is it that the young generation thinks being famous is won by becoming creative celebrities? Why not become famous by being a practical inventor?

You recalled a male artist, whom you admired not for his music only, but also for inspirational words he has for those aspiring to make a career in the music industry. He recently released a video which put you off. The female dancers twirled their half-naked bodies shamelessly, and their scantily-dressed bosoms reminded you of popping eyes. Meanwhile, he playfully slapped their bottoms. The women – not their acts – reminded you of Sara 'Saartjie' Baartman. Sara was considered a freak for having a large bottom and was put on display as a sexual curiosity. This same woman has become an icon, not only to her own Khoikhoi people, but to all women who know oppression and discrimination in their lives. So what creative art made anyone think it is graceful to inflict upon themselves what Sara went through?

You darted your eyes around the orange grove which was your afternoon haven. You hugged the thin stem, caressed the sunny ripened fruits, inhaled the white blossoms and thanked the anonymous farmer. The shiny green leaves reflected a smile for your gratitude. You remembered an incident. Two years ago you thanked all manual workers with these words, "Did you ever ask yourself if each one of us pursued a high educational degree, then who would do the skilled manual work? Craftsmanship may not earn us the money we want, but that does not mean we should lay scorn on anyone doing it. We are obliged to be respectful and grateful to anyone using their hands to clean our households, trim our hedges, construct our furniture, farm our food, craft the objects we collect and gift, style our hairs, etc. Next time you encounter a crafts person acknowledge their manual competence." Not everyone agreed with you. A person you knew confronted you, "I did not ask anyone to be a farmer. It was their choice to be one". This person had excelled in life from the earnings of parents who are farmers. Your answer was to repeat your gratitude again and again.

The Mind As A Beaver

Someday your mind will be a beaver:
terminating your existence at night
the mind role playing as a cleaver
gnawing your worth as it were a tree;
your creek turned to a brain fever
but not an end to the chaotic being
which you were its glorious weaver
pledged as the workaholic knight
whose mission now is a griever.

Jungle Of Life

In the jungle of muddled life
where predators are waiting
for your predicted fall,
you must choose to survive.

Claws of harsh judgement
from the wild kindred
tilting your gentle heart,
you must remain authentic.

Some growl their fancy feats
others howl in own demise
whether isolated or crowded,
you must stand out as unique.

There will be wild temptations
to glitter and glamour in labels
sealing low esteem of being,
you must live without pretence.

One peculiar day will arrive
when each animal is stripped
to reveal desire to be you,
you must portray humility.

In the jungle of serene life
where keepers are waiting
for your predicted rise,
you must choose to learn.

Life Is A Fortune Cookie

Forward ever, backward when there is a lion.
Walk with your head high and mind the bird droppings.
Do what you do worse and you will improve with time.

You are not alone asking for extra salt.
Drink a cup of jasmine tea and you will smell glorious.
Never let anyone come between you and eating a dessert.

This is a good time to get a heart break.
No, your bottom does not look like two stale biscuits.
The person you should marry is near you eating gooseberries.

Not all who pick their nose have lovely fingers.
Don't waste time asking questions, spend it being a question.
Tomorrow you will surprise everyone with a surprise.

A Litany Of Life

Whether in love or heart broken
the Earth will keep rotating to east.
Between your tears and laughter
the sun will always rise and set.
Beyond your joy and sorrows
the moon will always end up full.
Underneath the anger and hatred
love always lives in someone's heart
Blessed with light or cursed with dark
the stars will always glitter above.
Amongst the selfish and selfless
there will be prayers said to serve all.
Being defeated or having won battles
you will surrender to death someday.
Lived in sin or anointed in sainthood
someone will always remember you.

Party Under The Starry Night

I have placed my soul upon the starry night
stripping away the worries lived during day
and greet the dusking of another new night.

In the stillness of night
I cannot hear every sound whispered to me
yet music seeps through.

Thereby, I let body surrender melodic bones
of tiredness hanging in the closets of stress
where sneering floors are not invited to join.
I throw low esteem out.

From the party dress of my sequin soul
to never underestimate angelic presence
to lead beyond my humanly capabilities.

To be a song to each other
perfectly consoling yet of free will
my favourite conductors possibly unifying
with holiness full of beats and tempos.

Dancing
with electrifying swiftness of soul and spirit
to release its content of divine miracles
and unite with my inner self again.

I continue to write my composition
reliving abundance of melodious gifts
performing as strings across the sacred harp.

Graceful feet poised with confident steps
waltzing hope and gliding cure
from a few liberal stars on nursing gowns.

Every thought leads to glorious manifestation
and I will always receive greatness
with the best blueprints of affirmations.

To accept that my life isn't what your thoughts were.
Yet instead, has taught grand lessons even
to master plans from my own strategic mind.

Thankfully,
that although I will never shake hands with God
there's no denying the blessings of plans gone wrong.

Like A Shooting Star

They wouldn't take a moment and
notice you if it were not for your failures.
Choices of recklessness deep into madness
craving for eternal rise until heavenly portal opens.

Unending trials and sorrows
a unique stamp until that day of your glitter.
The fall of your wings buried in hopelessness
then found sacred distinction to stretch.

Despaired skies picked ascending star dusts
radiant of heavenly hope. Glorious dreams are not far.
There is only you of this kind. Remember your trueness.
Tomorrow is brighter if you dare lift your wings.

The light of eternity is dim without your glow.
Nothing that the Creator gave is of unworthiness.
Stop underestimating the heights of your light.
Rejoin the fleet of stars made of redemptive belief.

Understand the wealth of your dark moments and
embrace the call to shine light where impossible.
The glow of your will has catapulted and reached
wishes of the skies. Darkness came to reveal your light.

Divine time has come for you to land on greatness.
The skies are ready for you. Go forth and be one with it.
No curtain will dare shadow your determination.
You are a rare light. Rise and glitter like a shooting star.

Whenever your brilliance is shadowed, remember this: in every darkness, there is a light. Have a will to let go of your life's worries and sorrows. Give them up as a neat or shabby bundle. Burn them with meditation, prayers, kindness and/or creativity. Witness the ashes alter from weighed sadness to ballast hopefulness. Then, reclaim your rare light with redemptive acts. Sweep the floors of doubts. Wipe the low-spirited surfaces. Open the hidden godly windows. Keep going until all spaces are nothing but eternal glow of divine self.

A Flower In The Sky

You have always been a flower in the sky.
Flying to melodies of failed and triumphed life.
Today you are tested with plans gone wrong.
No metamorphosis prepared you for this trial.
Yet the music of change is calling you to dance.

You were egg, caterpillar, pupa and now butterfly.
Can you see transformation is a rhythm you know?
Do you remember stepping out from the cocoon?
Nobody could stop your tempo to aspired destiny.
Why let now taps of worries hinder your swing?

From today onwards the sky is your playground.
Swing to where you please not where despair calls.
Rave with your wings until clouds conspire to sing.
Be illuminating flower where it is least expected.
Spread magic of transformation to every dulled star.

Keep dancing whether in pristine or wild grounds.
You have always stood out as hard to pick flower.
So flutter, fly and float to the skies of hopefulness.
Wrap the music as you softly rest on shoulder of life.
Coz' nobody knows secrets of flowers like you do.

Some people are good at starting over. Others are terrible at starting over. And there are those who will simply not start over. This is poem is for all of us: the good, the terrible and the won't.

Keep Smiling

Smile until you sparkle night with your teeth,
and the distant planets applaud with a stand.

May your laughter fill Earth like happy Buddhas,
that those around you feel loveliness as green.

Cultivate your friendships slow as a sweet fruit,
just as you would always pray before you eat.

Trust that you have found true happiness, the
one we all want to sneak to our doors, don't we?

Never stop grinning even when it begins to spit.
Dance under the rain until your smile is back on.

Carve your reclaimed smile as emerald fire, and
shine light of your happiest spirit all the way out.

This poem is a golden shovel from Charles Simic's poem Watermelons.

She was laughing with her head
so I could not pull out her teeth.
Her laughter infected whoever came near.
I saw myself mirrored in her brown interior,
swarmed with bees spinning to a wind dance.
Her costume of yellow flair twirled on air,
as a goddess towing the sun on the ground.
The million laughing florets had me dare
to have faith in prayer in spite of tears.
I bowed my head to invoke a laughter,
and free my spirit to a dancing bee.

The Light In Your Darkness

I know too well –
the hollow darkness of despair,
the depth of hopelessness descend
which imprisons receipt of life's celebration,
and a cure of lasting acceptance.

There is little life without suffering
and no child can opt a return
to the womb of purity and innocence.
No bird hatches back to their egg
because once through the cracked door
there is no stepping back in
when you're already in the life.

In this doorway between Earth and Heaven
you must be alive, be grateful
only to erase your corroding hurt
before entering divine redemption.

A choir of celestial guardians
is gladly upon your watch
to convey chants of remarkable guidance
rather than explosions of accusing hymns.

And for those non-believers
who think their state is beyond rescue,
you still must feed, living
to the wet nurse of hope and patience.

For no matter your doubt
that no God could be witness
in this chaos full of misery,
feel then how it is
that angels live among the immoral
and the doomed.

Twinkles of the midnight stars,
reveries between light and dark
rejoice every dancing moment you're in,
living and wanting evermore.

Feel immensely blessed
for every unforeseen misfortune deed
which you have lived, thus keeping you busy
for several worthy living moments.

Rejoice in that one lasting night
to be led masterfully upon the floor
in the dance of life
with gratitude as your maid of honour.

Place your worries upon the dark night
and after it is gone, see the smiling moon
drawing back the curtain of its silky obscurity
to greet the arrival of sunny skies of hope.

How Can Each One Of Us Save The World?

Our twenty-first-century world is rich of humanitarian crises. Bodies are tainted with disasters. Minds are torn between right and wrong. Hearts are weeping from losses. Souls are haunted by injustices. As a citizen, there are ample issues to demonstrate against. All around you, someone you know or heard of is doing something to save humanity.

You, on the other hand, might have recoiled to a hopeless state, believing that you lack the voice or an established platform to be heard. Perhaps you have chosen to guard yourself with a protection bubble of familiarity. Whatever you choose to do or not, you, too, matter.

To save the world, it is a requisite to adhere to our most basic universal human values. We need people who harness action against those who stray from them. We also need people who continue to instil these values every single day, whether through practises and creations which teach and uplift others or reaching out to those who are alone in their maladies. They are all equally important in the quest of a peaceful world.

You can opt to remain calm between the chaos and drama, if that's what you are comfortable with. Maybe being out there in the action crushes your highly sensitive self. While others are demonstrating, it's all right to be quiet and take care of yourself. Don't be guilt-ridden when others are working to reveal and boycott the misdeeds of others. They need you to balance their energy of action. You want to be a better person, not a bitter one.

If you choose to demonstrate against, do it peacefully. If you choose to stay put, create or do what would nourish a soul. The world needs both extinguishers of darkness and matchsticks of light. You can choose to be any of them or both.

Now go in peace and save our world.

A Family Riddle

Between mother and father
I don't know
who is helpless.

She prays that he returns
even with aftertaste of
other women.

He brings to her crevices
sated secretions from
other women.

The Almost Holy Quaternity

The three of us
we were an ideal family
I thought.

We looked happy
with puffed up cheeks and
semi-circled lips.

But where were you?
Not a shadow or outline in
that sepia portrait.

Were you the photographer
or the stranger visiting us
moments later?

Mother, sister, brother
that holy trinity missed you
our father.

We would have been
the idolised quaternity of
my family.

Revelation

It was a month before Christmas and you were gifted a revelation: complete as an Advent wreath with its four candles of hope, peace, joy, and love. You have watched him given a life three times before, and this was the fourth.

Hope was when God created him as an answer to a prayer for a son. Thereafter, his mother made a promise not to have another child. A prayer was kept on a door for those who lived in the house and visitors to witness that solemn promise. He was named Emmanuel. He was a fine boy until he became ill. A condition that no doctor understood, they gave up on him. Anyone involved in his care got tested. Nights became a drilling exercise against peace. When others went to sleep, you watched her start the night as day, by lulling him to sleep. You wanted to reach out and help. What was he afraid of? But, as soon as dawn came, he became peaceful again. You were too small to understand. So you resorted to silent vows of protecting him like a big sun. Peace hugged you after accepting his nights as days. He was your light brother.

One day his illness was gone. It happened without medication. You continued life, at times stopping to smile and laugh at his joyful acts. You oozed with pride as he intoxicated joy to friends and small children. He shared what he had – food, clothes and even kind words. He was a glory to behold when he shared his best clothes with a friend or, when he rewarded sweets from his shop to school children after completing their homework. You marvelled at the bold courage he had to inspire a child to walk, and conquer a perceived disability. You were too caught at his given joys and failed to see him fight for life, until he made a plunge to a dark world of substance abuse. You noticed after his plea for help. That was the fourth time.

You begged him to recall his magical recovery from the unknown illness. He listened and mended for a short duration, before surrendering to darkness again. After the whys and hows have been asked, you prayed that he finds love. A love even you were tempted not to give, as you sought to understand his purpose in life. Then you understood. He was here to give you four lessons: hope, peace, joy, and love on life. He was a son of hope, a brother of your peace and kindness for your joy. Now, have courage and love him again.

An Easter Prayer

It was Easter day, the day of hope and forgiveness. The man she was to celebrate that day was her saviour Jesus Christ, nailed upon a cross for acts he committed not. However, reflection of that selfless act made her recall not the son of God.

One of them betrayed her with many affairs. Another was secretly married while having a relationship with her. And there was one who physically abused her. And another who raped her. Tears rolled down her face. She was carrying a cross of past pains. Which God created such men? She wanted to exhaust fear from those who hurt her. Being reborn with forgiveness seemed a far-flung possibility, just as was Christmas day in April. She needed to love again until the last drop of water and blood drained out of her, as it did Jesus when pierced both sides.

She walked to the bedroom and recalled moments before making love. A naked body is pathway to a naked soul. If those men have seen her that way, so shall her God, too. She undressed and touched lovingly every contour of her body until compassion for her naked body took over. Then she knelt down to say a prayer.

Almighty God, I was born naked to a precious gift of life. Help me embrace that gift again with full love of my body, including the relationship scars it bears. God, I was out yesterday walking in the forest, speaking to the trees and praying for a sign that you were listening to my prayers. I saw none except for a shadow of trees following me as ghosts of my former lovers. Please help me appreciate men again. Help me shine a light of love towards every man I meet today and days to come. God, I know there is a very thin line between a believer, an evangelist and a fanatic. Please guide me against imposing my beliefs on others and help me realise when needed to serve as an example to humanity. I am not done with learning, so please remind me always, that regardless of how others treat me, we are all from one God, including right now when I find it difficult to accept that those who hurt me are from the same God. In the name of almighty Father, ascended masters, angel men and good spirited men. Amen.

She stood up and faced a holy cross that was pinned above her dresser. Humming hallelujah, she swayed from side to side. She hymned until her naked spirit was full of love for men again. That night she dreamt of a handsome loving man.

Sabbatical Kiss

His mouth recited
prayers and hymns.
I dared kiss him
to purify my poetry.

In The Aquamarine Of This Day

You are a laughing angelate in the aquamarine of this day,
careless, yet promising like a healer's gold on sinned chest
unwrapping me from the green of owned envious malachite.

You made of ancient ochre skilfully wrapped as amber knows
this pure day could end in the melancholy of garnet on ground
or sparkly of holy lights; as if sky was dotted in endless quartz.

You say, "I am here to crystallise your soul worthy as a stone".
I wonder how on Earth your digging tools will manage that
without killing the purity hidden as unpolished ghastly onyx.

You open me with tenderness of ruby found untainted afar
yet closer as turquoise seeking to be found in the wings of love
buried deeply as blue opal waiting to rise as crystal for fortune.

You, from the kingdom of copal fossilized as dear warmth
release my deadness concealed in the interior as false ruby
turning this day to a sunny night adorned with gem's rarities.

A Simple Touch

You need not invade my privacy.
A reach with your hands
and I recover. With a simple touch.

Should you want to dare
gaze into my lonely eyes
and help me unload burdens.

Do not waver. Hold me steadily.
Gift me endless dreams
seen in the bloom of your iris.

I am neither the sky
nor the stars which glitter across it.
And when, at last, our fusion
is let go by flicking images.

Your caressing touch
is still felt even when gone:
uplifting me to perpetual heights
of glorious divine company.

Where stars of comradeship
seem far to reach
in the hollows of lonesomeness,
come again, and again.

It's in your compassion self
to never let me suffer alone.
Touch me again.
Yes, touch me once more.

The Vows

Eros swore to celibacy
the moment I fell in love.

I made him swear –

to want me
when my yearning slanted
like drunken trees in winter,

to adore me
when my curves deformed
like a novice in pottery class,

to love me
when my body oversized
like winner of scratch fight,

to cherish me
when my twos drooped
like lemons in the socks.

He was not Eros
and gladly kept the vows.

Affirmations

Squash me to small pieces
and I will rise
into fine symphony.

Humiliate me to non-existence
and I will surpass
into vibrant bloom.

Ignore me to unknown soul
and I will shine
into glorious being.

Love me like you do
and I will bloom to be
queen of all flowers.

An innocent presence
my reminder of rape.

I spread my legs not once
but many times.

They slipped out of me
unwanted and unloved.

Then I went to church
and prayed for forgiveness.

The Wedding Speech

Wedding speech had her query living vows in make good
as the speaker insisted that nothing is best than motherhood.

Some think of crafting and conquering during girlhood
while others relive trauma and miseries from childhood.

No child is a sacrifice akin the acts of deserved sainthood
and neither is child raising a token of great womanhood.

The assumption every woman wants it is falsehood
and it was enough fire to make the bride's limbs stood.

To the shock of everyone, the bride made herself understood
that procreating is not what she wants in life as a do good.

Unfortunate the majority of listeners chose to misunderstood
her reasoning as the wicked deed to outcast from sisterhood.

A Woman's Inferno

In the core of her delightful laughter
she exhaled darkness of her sufferings
and it made her glow with superiority.

She danced in her shoes of troubles
shook her waist in devilish swirls, and
vibrated her hips in angelic swings.

The queen of once glorious paradise
daylight gave in to her grief command
as she spurted agonies into the clouds.

Hell and heaven met in the galaxy
of sorrows woven in hairy predicament
and cathartic thrusts of endless storm.

The king of mental and physical abuses
wooed her to the bed of desperate debris
until she was nothing but raging inferno.

Finally, she settled on canvas of hope
split her womb open with daring pride
and bred offspring of blissful melancholy.

The Heart Is Never Yours

It was yours since you first tasted air and
screamed furiously for warmth.

Loving hands abundant with closeness
wrapped you in fluffy care all day and night.

For many years it was yours only until
the day you encountered that feeling.

The screams which never failed to give you
everything desired didn't work.

The designed chambers to keep you alive with
food and water longed for a stranger.

The relaxing and contracting thuds of your
vitality called their name.

The stranger appeared and took it away for
their intimate collection.

You tried to get it back. It was returned
full of markings from touch.

Do you realise now that it was never yours
from the beginning of life?

You were just a nurturer of
what would belong to someone else.

Single And Beautiful

Christmas season had arrived and you fretted over it. It was a time where you as a single mother were frowned upon. Your fatherless children, they, too, got their share of sneers for not having received expensive gifts from both parents. None of this was your wish, but it had happened. He left you after bearing your second child. You never got to commit marital vows. Your pride guided you to wait and be wooed, and later asked for your hand. He never got to the latter.

You loved flowers, especially lilies. One evening after returning from work, a two-weeks-old withered bouquet of pink lilies welcomed you. With a heavy heart – because you knew it would be a while until you could afford another – you made way to the organic bin. Then you noted one unopened bloom. Spontaneously, you plucked it off from the rest and placed it in a drinking glass half-filled with water. This simple arrangement centred your kitchen table. Then you gathered your children in the kitchen. That evening before dinner you asked them to note the unopened flower. Next day after returning from work, you gathered your children in the kitchen again. You asked them to note the language of the flower. In a modest way it spoke, "I am single and beautiful." Your children were impressed with the unforgettable statement of simplicity and elegance.

A year later, Christmas knocked on the door. Your money savings didn't suffice to buy a tree, a splashy meal and gifts for your children. As you were mulling over going to the bank to ask for increase of your credit limit, your children walked in your bedroom. They noted that something was not right and asked you. However, you chose to say you were feeling unwell. The next morning you found your children up and seated in the kitchen. When you asked what the matter was, they simply said, "Mommy, this year we don't want any gifts or a Christmas tree." Your heart palpated. Maybe they wanted something more expensive. How could you afford a tropical holiday? The best you could do was a beach visit at a nearby river. You wished children didn't tell each other so much about their holidays. Your reeling thoughts were interrupted. "We just want a single lily in the kitchen."

That night you wanted to pray and praise every celestial being. But you knew there was one, who particularly deserved this grace. Archangel Gabriel is God's Holy Messenger. Gabriel is usually depicted holding a lily, which stands for purity and truth. And on this night, the bearers of Gabriel's message were your children. Beauty was what they saw through you. You knelt down and honoured the precious duty of being a single mother.

When A Pleasure Giver Siezes Your Body

And when a pleasure giver last arrives
to seize your body with doings,
you must give in.
You have been innocent and unaware,
a maiden to ways of bodily pleasure.
Respond not joyfully,
to hasty direct manoeuvres,
that seduce your body not,
to eloquent state of being wanted.
Until wantonly treatment is guaranteed,
no soul should be granted a lesson,
even a holder of PhD in heavenly satisfaction.
Never admit to knowing nothing.
You know how to be treated.
Finally that time to be worshiped arrives,
go through it only when feeling ready.
Invite the deserved to your hidden petals,
fear not the nectarine applaud of your temple.
(Unite)
You might meet your Creator with your mouth,
as you sing praises to your pleasure giver.
God is there alright, dwelling
with every breath and pant you make.
Thank him, for showing you love
disguised in an unruly act.
Be grateful for being brave
where regrets are not welcomed.
You have galloped to womanhood.
Emerge head held high.

The Fruit

That pear-shaped thing I owned
cost family a lot of prayers.
Their hope ridden as Noah's arc
by sick and maddening liquids.
They disguised its assured death
with novenas, hymns and fasting.

It assumed surface of custard apple.
Nodules filled with sterile flesh
pushing and suffocating other things
to a mass of irk gluing and bloating.

The undertaker came unannounced.
Two dead seeds were drilled out of it.
They still prayed, prayed and prayed.
God wouldn't listen to any of it.
He was right – for being told how to.

To avoid litany, I killed the fruit in secrecy.
Another tree offered me one of its seed.
I gladly took it to the shock of my family.
But the angels jubilated my boldness
coz' they knew that seed needed my soil.

Elegy For Unborn Child

You who were guarded by angels
lived and let go after a few weeks.
I write about you to not grieve
the short memories with a heave.

In my verses you span every page
pleading for after wisdom as a sage.
You came to life as a joy conceived
and left behind a mother bereaved.

You weren't here but we spoke
the womb guarding like a cloak.
The miracle of fecundity came
and we were choosing a name.

You were too young to declare
that life is not without a tear.
And so I shall pen your hours
as a unicorn galloping to ours.

I will offer thanksgiving
for your coming and short living,
coz' no moment was a procrastination
as you seized the glory of creation.

The full moon calls:
mighty warrior souls,
break chains of doubts.

We are all angelic.
Offspring of godly relic,
accept and be prophetic.

Gather for a singspiel.
Our angel is Gabriel.
Our angel is Gabriel.

Embrace the divine sight.
Bathe in purity of night.
Be one with moonlight.

Full Moon Release

You stared towards a window. That window in your attic bedroom has always been your sanctuary for admiring a full moon. Yesterday you were too occupied. Today, as you were about to go to bed, you saw it peeking through the peaks of tall trees. It was the biggest you had seen this year. Instead of wishing, you remembered.

A doctor's visit confirmed you were pregnant. It was against your teachers' and parents' teachings. Motherhood was too early for you. You had to build your career first. So you found another doctor to help you abort it. A life was lost. Years passed until you were ready.

A doctor's visit confirmed no heart beats. It was against your motherhood plans. You had to try again. So you found doctors to help you keep it. Still, a life was lost. These trials repeated countless times until you had no choice but to accept the losses. Your acceptance involved asking the Holy Mother to convey a wish to God – angels come to help you take the small one's life out of you gently. Maybe it wouldn't hurt so much. As you prayed, you saw flying shadows above you. You silently spoke, "Thank you for being here and help me take it away peacefully." Then you gave up on trying ever again.

A forest visit changed your life. It was there that you asked your children's spirits to rest in peace. A white feather landed on your shoulder. You took it as a sign that God has forgiven you. Amidst your cries and sorrows was a man. He loved you unconditionally. His love was so big that it brought you guilt instead of joy. One day you stared out of the window and saw a full moon. You became obsessed by the lunar object. It saw your worries, fear and guilt. The moon wished to dispel all these, only if you asked. But you didn't dare ask.

One spring evening, he joined you and said, "Make a wish. It's magical to wish on the full moon."

I wish to the moon that I accept my fate.
I also wish to feel deserving of this man's love.
I also wish –
for a healthy body, peace of mind, a forgiving heart, and kind spirit.

The moon accepted your wishes.

In the silence of the night, where serenity blanketed the world, you both howled from the union of your bodies. The full moon exposed your raw needs. You wanted nothing but to be ravished under the exposure of the full moon. You begged him to touch, in and out of your ample femininity. Before the moon bid farewell, you swore to grant it imprints of your passionate acts.

The moon applauded.

The Chronicles Of A Redeemed Life

I.
An elusive condition
it was a vision of false diagnosis:
fibroids.

The body became a riddle.
Is it bloated?
Is it sick?
Is it aged?
Is it normal?

The wardrobe
was opulent with disguises:
bigger panties
oversized fashion
maternity outfits.

Travelling and outing
the reasons to petrify as follows:
regular stops
frequent changing
repeated winces.

Love suffered
from painful sex
and infertility.

After poking and thrusting
after cutting and stitching
after healing and scarring
we don't know had a name –
adenomyosis.

II.
Bracing up for the raw pain
from cuts between chest and hip
I sat up to listen to
the cries of new arrivals.

Meanwhile
the body cured of a malady
which threatened comforts of life;
it was no occasion for bitterness
to hear them throughout the night.

They kept crying
not for me
the woman without a womb.

I cried too
for a belly I cannot have
and sounds I cannot birth.

III.
Then I met
the sister of the sun and
the night goddess.

One grieving night
she invited me to
bashes of housekeeping.

At the new moon party to
claim the broom of acceptance.

At the crescent gathering to
sweep the grimy floors of fears.

At the quarter get-together to
wipe all the low-spirited surfaces.

At the waxing festivities to
clean all the dusty godly windows.

At the full moon celebration to
rise again like a shooting star.

And so I kept going
until the day I felt the moon
become my new womb.

I was pregnant
with divine light.

Purity Came

Purity came.
She was small with big intentions.
Why do you forget who you are?
She asked, as I was about to weep.
So the tears streamed back
to the lake of memories.

I was without a home
to host her for nine months.
But she was here waiting for me.
What did she want?

She said, a poem and a story.
And so I became the mother
who nurtured her imagination.
I cared from a distance as a writer
but she knew I loved her.

That Gloomy Day

What was to be her gloomy day became vibrant.
Oh, look! It was an epistle of sketches and colours.
Climbing back upstairs felt like a sinking elephant.
She collected what was in the door mailbox.
The sun looked worried as a bride on first night.
Trees lost their spring blooms as if in autumn.
Grey clouds gathered for a day's congregation.
She went out to rearrange the fallen flower pots.
Outside the house were sounds of melancholy.

* *This poem tells a story backwards.*

You Came Looking For Mother

All the water in rivers and oceans
all the trees standing tall and free
all the blooms on ground and air,

I was there.

I was the water gushing from the womb
I was the food while bleeding on moss
I was the epiphany of the mother goddess.

My grounds are sacred venues of life
there you have been alive than above
as you crawled, walked and stumbled.

I let you trample life on my surfaces
I let you plant and reap as you please
I let you drill me to depths of miseries.

There is a reason you came looking
nothing surges ahead without living
coz' nobody knows you like a mother.

Awaken in deference to your soul and spirit
for without them you are a covenant of putrid.
Grant me your worship in all forms of life.
Do you want your mother goddess again?

When The Ocean Kisses

I will drown! I will rise!
This is the sinking woman
whose soul touched the ocean and
caused it to storm kisses.
A wave caresses.
Another wave caresses.
Embrace the water.
Flood despair with hope.
Rise.
Rise higher.
The ocean kisses!

*This poem is inspired by the haka dance lyrics.

The Wild Woman

There is a call from the frightened place
daring my scared feet to feel the wet mud
running to where the moon flirts with bare skin
and walking a path caressed by uncombed hair.

A dwelling where rules and walls disappear
except stories, poetry and songs of the spirit
bones freed of fearful and belittling shackles
a soul in charge of its own dance through life.

Tonight I will get out and run to the woods
to bathe full moon and rid of my shadows
to sing and recite until fear accept defeat
then return home with knowing how to flee

Starry Bliss

The soul is a star
at the centre of the Solar System.
It is often said that the soul is
an "ordinary" star.
In truth, the soul is a magnetically
active star.
Sometimes the moon comes
between it and the Earth.
When lined up perfectly
the stars come out.
The animals and birds think
it's time to sleep.
When gone
we still have moon and stars.
For humans
a worth starry bliss.

On The Stairway To Paradise

It is a sunny day in December. Your thirty-fifth birthday is in twenty days. You have no plans to celebrate at all. Instead you find yourself day dreaming in a Mexican cemetery, fascinated by thoughts of death. Ahead of you is the Bridge to Paradise, made out of a cone with seven levels representing the days of the week and three-hundred-and-sixty-five tombs on the outside depicting the days in the year. Your feet begin ascending the stairway to paradise. It's a path bearing fifty-two steps; symbolising the weeks in a year. Time and death are intertwined. Then you remembered.

Twenty-five years ago, on a sunny day similar to this you were sent for an afternoon nap. Your house help, Saida, followed you to the room. Her duty as usual was to make sure you take that nap. She smears your feet with a thick layer of Vaseline. Nothing is suspicious to you. Next, she lies next to you, her head opposite yours. She takes your left leg and places it between her thighs. She grinds herself with it. You try to stop as your feet gets hotter and your leg numb from being in the same position for too long. She holds your feet and pressed harder on herself. You cannot sleep because she makes strange noises. It will stop after she makes that one particular sound. You do not know what it means, but you have come to accept this ritual every naptime.

You beg the spirits to forgive your dirty memories.

The personal references on the graves catch your attention: a boat, a baby angel, a tilted pot, etc. Here are spirits from all ages, social classes and names. There is no separation. Like you, they have lived and sinned. Some might have confessed and others not. What matters is what they liked. A knowing embraces you. It's not yet time for paradise. You must descend back to the living. Then you remembered.

A year ago, you met a woman. You were attending a women's workshop in Lagos.
She said, "I would like to kiss you."
You replied, "Please do."
You meekly followed her to the ladies' toilet. There she kissed you
passionately. You responded naively. Thereafter with each lead, she aroused
your secret. You have been there before with your imaginations.

At the bottom of Bridge of Paradise, you find a circular cave beckoning
with flickering candles. In there you collapse in front of a Madonna statue,
surrounded by a complete circle of candles and shrines. Your secret is safe
with the spirits. Return to life with no regrets.

Words In The Silence

A knot tied hard
inside a woman's womb
rippling her insides
with waves of nausea
and other panic attacks.

In the silence is a conversation
between angels and devils
one that is so holy
that nothing else matters
except worship its words
until she finds
her sacred path again.

We stand for trust
assured the angels.
We stand for doubt
affirmed the devils.
I stand to decide
uttered the modest she.

There is nothing befriending like solitude.
Conversing with the invisible:
fallen ancestors, angels and even stars.

Behold the comradeship given, once you
know this fleet of quiet friends. The joyful
moments from noisy chaos is endless.

Fear not the introverted space. There you will
meet adventures your soul seeks. Write, paint, pray
or do nothing. Allow yourself divine purification.

Meet your spirit in the silence – wildly or godly.
Unlock your lost self in empowering bliss. Forget
sneers from others. They only fear your trueness.

Return to them with luminous acceptance of
yourself. Grace your being with an ear of its soul.
There is nothing befriending like your own you.

Under The Mango Tree

You sat under the mango tree and shook your head with disbelief. The argument given for condemning the person whose sexuality did not fit the assigned categories of female or male originated from religious reasons.

The accused was indicted for practicing behaviour from the western world. That it was a sin according to the holy book. Where did that holy book come from? Where did that religion come from? Was it not from the western world?

Before religion made its way where the accused live, what did they practise? Did their tradition condemn this behaviour? Did the old belief recognise that there are women who are better off being husbands? Did it witness that there are men who had rather be wives? How did their cultural practise sort this need?

Did the elders shut their eyes and let it stream to the next generation without explanation? Did they allow it but discreetly? Did they rearrange communal practises to cater the needs for those who do not fit the clear-cut gender? Or did they perform a mass of bodily correcting operations?

If condemning today one who uses not the right hand as backwards and outdated, why not the same for one who feels not clear cut male or female?

Everyone deserved to sit under a mango tree and think not of where they fit sexually. There they would pick a fruit of their choice–ripe, unripe or half ripe. What mattered was the tree did not choose who sat under it. It gave freely of its succulent gifts to sate the need of everyone. The tree never asks if you are a farmer or not. It doesn't interrogate whether you contributed in the cultivation of its growth or not. The fruits hang at different heights. It's up to you to reach where you can. When the fruit season is over, it still provides with protection against scorching heat or thunder pour.

You thanked the tree for offering an isolated and peaceful shade for you to contemplate. Then you prayed for the condemned person to see fruity days in the remainder of their exposed life.

In Our Souls Is A Rainbow

We are a rainbow.

Each one a colour,
our differences only two,
a primary or secondary.

In the arc is our bow,
representing all colours,
at the centre of love.

Our mission is one,
painting others hearts,
with colourful deeds.

In the sun of our laughter,
and rain of our tears,
there will be a rainbow.

The sun shall obediently,
illuminate our intentions,
to paint worries with light.

Amidst hardship trials,
we will remember,
in our soul lives a rainbow.

And with every step,
let we be remembered,
for our colourful trails.

A rainbow is we.

You did not know him. In fact, you did not know him until you met. Then you wondered, if you knew him or not. Growing up, nobody mentioned him. But he was there. Living life invisibly, or else be ridiculed mercilessly. Neither your parents nor anyone else with a role to guide you in life had mentioned about him. So, how can it be that years later you learned that he was taboo?

The first time you met him, it was confusion between accepting him wholly yet unsure of what you have accepted. Your instincts guided you as a kind person yet there was a peculiar awkwardness of the unknown. But life had long ago taught you to seek information in order to make sound judgement. So you asked. How he loved. How he did it. How he felt. There were more questions and he was more than happy to clarify. Then you became friends. Your friendship became trusting. That's when you knew you have known him all along. You too have been there.

You were there when he was confused about his feelings. You were there when his heart fluttered because he was in love. You were there when he first kissed. You were there when he was in a steady relationship. You were there when he worried about welfare of his lover. You were there when he needed to confide secrets during a beauty session. You were there when next day he could not stop smiling because yesterday was so great. You were there when he wept for days over a broken heart. You were there when he picked up the broken pieces and started all over. So how can he be a taboo?

How can he be a forbidden subject if what he does is nothing but seek love? We all want to be loved. How can that be wrong? You decided to dive into the deep end and ask your mother. Her frankness surprised you. She has never considered asking. You both took a long pause. Then she asked if you knew. Together while seated on wooden stools, facing a charcoal stove while cooking ugali, you began narrating. You did not hold back and neither did she. The more you told, the more she asked. That's when you realised she knew him too.

If you knew him and so did your mother, is it possible that others knew him, too, but dared not ask? And if it were so, how could others be encouraged to realise that they, too, know him? This truth seemed a fruit too high up the tree to pick. Until that happens, you were determined to set a rippling action to end phobia towards him. Be an example to others and accept him. Then someday, others will recognise they, too, know him.

Calming The Qualms

Gently you prodded me
to let go of my fears in the vibrant African sunrise.

Gracefully you taught me
to walk worldly plains in elegant giraffe strides.

Proudly you urged me
to own my inner self as confident lion paws.

Masterfully you coached me
to revive my greatness as the Kilimanjaro height.

Wisely you encouraged me
to admire other souls as a radiant rainbow.

Boldly you asked me
to calm my qualms in the grand African sunset.

Be still.
The river calls for your divine calm.
Do you have the will to hear it?

The sand and pebbles attune to you.
There is a song awaiting your listening.
Can you dare to receive its calling?

The silence might awaken your demons.
They will rob your spirit of its unfolding.
Will you let your peace flow upstream?

Be still.
Though deeply submerged you're still fine.
Do you know that to live without persistence is to die?

Something Marvelous Is Waiting
To Happen On Monday

Four decades ago, a Tanzanian woman decided to mop the floor of her two-bedroom house. Meanwhile, her belly began contracting. She went ahead with cleaning the floor. Her waters broke. She was rushed to hospital and had a healthy baby girl. It was Monday and the last day of the year.

Years later, that baby girl grew and migrated to Ireland for further studies. After completion of her first degree, she moved on to study, live and work in Germany. Her recollection of memories cannot point to the exact time she heard of Monday blues. Nevertheless, she is here to make the case for Monday.

For many around the world, 16 January is Blue Monday and the saddest day of the year. This day was created in 2005 by a British holiday company. Many take the opportunity to advise on how to live the supposedly saddest day. This credence of sadness and unhappiness has spilled over to all Mondays. Advocated by pseudoscience, Monday is tainted with thoughtless words and negative clichés. Quotes and sayings have been created for it: even the sun must be saying, 'oh, no it's Monday'; may your coffee be strong and your Monday short; if it had a face I would punch it; why is it so far from Friday; it's Doomsday; not enough coffee can help you; keep calm and pretend it's not Monday; etc.

I am that baby girl who was born on Monday. There wouldn't be life for me if it were not for Monday. The day is assigned to Archangel Gabriel. This messenger angel helps others and me to be messengers ourselves, writer, musician, artist, journalist or teacher. I hold dear the day this angel gently nudged me to sit down and let the pen speak for me. I was a furious soul and full of hate. I wondered, "How possibly could a human bear so much hate on other like what I feel right now?" Memories of good times were erased with bad times. The potential greatness of a human was blinded with a list of mistakes. I didn't care of any amount of goodness that a human was capable of. Benevolence was overwhelmed with a fury that threatened to damage myself and the offender. The screams in my soul threatened to obscure the light of my spirit. So I sat down and wrote. It was the first and longest poem I ever wrote. I channelled all my hate to that longest verse until was exhausted of abhorrence. The ten reasons why I hated were penned down. It was the beginning of my forgiving and writing journey.

Today Monday remains a special day. It is a day where I affirm greatness to be had for the entire new week. It is a day where I am the most creative and courageous to share my thoughts in writing. It is a gifted day to start afresh and toss away the mourning as if doomsday. I embrace the day as a second shoe until I am done walking the thrills. It is a wonderful day that no taints from negative clichés shall surpass my highest regard of it. It is holy because there are no blues in my Mondays, just ample hues of different blessings.

There will be no joyful week without Monday. Whether it is a writing feast day or a lesson to correct past mistakes, there is greatness waiting to happen and endorse the brilliance of this glorious day. I am delighted for Monday to come.

Monday Hues

When light gilds over the seven hills
sculpting them to gliding ocean waves
I greet this new day with gratitude
and affirm greatness to be achieved.

That Monday is a gift to start afresh
I toss away the mourning as if doomsday
and embrace the day as my second shoe
until we are done walking the thrills.

Whether coiffured with vexing routine
or farfetched wild weekend fantasies
my resurrection isn't a distant hope
because of this new beginnings day.

If divine Monday doesn't come round
surely I won't survive rest of the week.
Coz' there are no blues in my Mondays
just ample hues of possible blessings.

Praise without doubt, for I have seen
signs and messages from celestial beings.
It began on April night, two years ago.
Whether a dream, vision or thought
a thirst to find the divine self-persisted.
Something occurred to heal my soul.

A soul flooded with regrets and sorrows
it began with a loud help to the holiest.
I was heard by the guardians on Earth — angels.
Then I met forgiveness and endless love.
I believe.

Reclaiming My Angels

Every day of the week
I failed to see blessings
radiating in different strengths.

On Sunday,
I am protected through Michael.
On Monday,
strength rules in me through Gabriel.
On Tuesday,
my path is guarded through Raphael.
On Wednesday,
wisdom pours in me through Uriel.
On Thursday,
kindness touches me through Sachiel.
On Friday,
my grace lasts through Jehudiel.
On Saturday,
blessings are with me through Barachiel.

Every day of the week,
I failed to see revelations,
in different symbols.

When a third eye told me not to
Michael's blue guards my path.
When battling with sickness
Raphael's green heals me.
When my soul writes
Gabriel's white reveals greatness to me.
When calm amidst a storm
Uriel's red grants me wisdom.
When awed with dark thoughts
Jophiel's yellow beautifies my world.
When boiling with revenge
Zadkiel's purple awards me forgiveness.
When feeling the butterflies
Chamuel's pink rewards me pure love.

All along
you've been there,
yet I failed to see you.
Thank you Chamuel,
and fellow guardian angels,
for helping me find
what I had lost
a long while ago.

Angelic Flurries

Angels are all around us
and I saw one yesterday.
You may try to repress
angels are all around us.
I wish to confess
they are still there today.
Angels are all around us
and I saw one yesterday.

Wings Of Aurora

Now I know the reason for those blessed dreams
floating heaven with clouds as climbing beams
where fear and threat are thwarted by great abilities
and soaring visions dwell with mighty possibilities.

I am the wings of Aurora flying to greater heights
come join me and the elves in the waves of sprites
we say no to our doubts and yes to spiritual truth
together we rise high to the enriched path of sooth.

I shall play no more small to that brings me down
farewell descending shoes hello ascending crown
time has come to light up examples of inspiration
I thank my angels with pretty garland of carnation.

This poem is inspired by the angel oracle card Aurora.

The Mindfulness Creed

I believe in mindfulness,
the awareness needed,
as the foundation of the present.
I believe in non-judgement, for my well-being.
All experiences are the same,
whether suffering or delighting,
under spiritual attention,
they bring fulfilment, here and now.
Before sinking into stress,
rise I will into equanimity.
I believe in patience,
in listening,
in acceptance,
in letting go,
and in fully being myself.
Namaste.

Acknowledgements

The author would like to thank the editors of the following periodicals and festival platform where some of these poems first appeared.

1. A Simple Touch. *SIBYL Magazine:* For the Spirit and Soul of Woman.
2. An Easter Prayer. *SIBYL Magazine:* For the Spirit and Soul of Woman.
3. Calming the Qualms. *When Women Waken,* A Journal of Poetry, Prose & Images by Women.
4. Forbidden Thoughts. *SIBYL Magazine:* For the Spirit and Soul of Woman.
5. Gratitude Beneath an Orange Grove. *SIBYL Magazine:* For the Spirit and Soul of Woman.
6. Like a Shooting Star. *SIBYL Magazine:* For the Spirit and Soul of Woman.
7. Our Pact. *When Women Waken,* A Journal of Poetry, Prose & Images by Women.
8. Party Under the Starry Night. *SIBYL Magazine:* For the Spirit and Soul of Woman.
9. Single and Beautiful. *SIBYL Magazine:* For the Spirit and Soul of Woman.
10. The Almost Holy Quaternity. *WILDsound Writing Festival,* a monthly writing festival performed by professional actors.
11. The Mindfulness Creed. *When Women Waken,* A Journal of Poetry, Prose & Images by Women.
12. When a Pleasure Giver Seizes Your Body. *When Women Waken,* A Journal of Poetry, Prose & Images by Women.
13. When the Ocean Kisses. *When Women Waken,* A Journal of Poetry, Prose & Images by Women.
14. Wings of Aurora. *When Women Waken,* A Journal of Poetry, Prose & Images by Women.
15. Wisdom of Living Water. *When Women Waken,* A Journal of Poetry, Prose & Images by Women.

Thank you for buying and reading this book. I wish to have written you a personal note of gratitude. Nevertheless, I hope you feel gifted with an inside peek to my thoughts and feelings.

If you liked this book, please write a review on Amazon or Goodreads. Your feedback will help me to serve you with more good writing.

Also, I thank you in advance for recommending or sharing with someone else. What good use is knowledge obtained from a book if it remains hidden in a book shelf?

Explore Poetry And Prose From Other Collections

Mists of Sense Require Fierce Poesy. This poetry book takes readers into miracles of embracing oneself as divine being; adulthood and its dilemmas, troubles and heartaches; and national identity, broken homelands with violence and destruction of land and human spirit. However, the human spirit is resilient. So I hope at the end readers will celebrate with me the winning attitudes with triumphs over trials. Summed up in a sentence: the book dares you to emerge with a kind heart: despite the thickness of the mist, the pride you will have displayed, the tears you will have shed, the rants you will have made, the fierce poems you will have written and winning attitudes you will have dared.

The Wisdom Huntress. This book takes the reader along a ride through cultural familiarities as experienced by the narrator Savannah, all the while passing by liminal experiences that illustrate the importance of being receptive and open-minded in an ever-shrinking world. The book also provides an opportunity to introduce the African proverbs and Kanga sayings, to those not acquainted with them. The book is presented in a very non-linear progressive manner, opening and closing chapters with a new theme and lesson in mind. Each chapter has its own unique story and purpose, but they all aim together toward the same goal – the acquisition and distribution of wisdom. After experiencing joyous love and heartaches, insecurities and swelling pride, abuses and tender reinforcements, the narrator comes out of the callous jungle of life on top, roaring her victorious cries over the plains of Africa.

Mahaba Prints in My Heart. This anthology of poetry about facets of good love – desire, friendship, fantasy, naughtiness, passion, patience, purity, sultriness, temptation and other unnamed, was written during a difficulty time. Whilst undergoing a divorce, I published a book of love poetry. Thankfully, the book helped me to not abandon the idea of falling in love again. It was a sort of therapy after an ending of a love relationship. The book aided me with courage to see the love I have had to that point of my life.

Gloria D. Gonsalves, also fondly known as Auntie Glo, is a multi-published author. She likes to dwell on different themes inspired by human and natural worlds. However, deep down she knows that spirit and soul will always provide writing prompts if she cares to listen. When taking a break from writing, she creates micropoems and quotes.

Not just a writer, Gloria is a creative promoter for writing itself: she founded WoChiPoDa.com, an initiative aimed at instilling the love of poetry in young people.

Gloria was born and raised in Tanzania. She is currently based in Germany having previously lived in Ireland.

Made in the USA
Monee, IL
15 February 2022

91325740R00059